_____ Get

Cassandra,

Always put wings to your dreams! I believe in "You"

Tyrone Lister

Praise For Getting Back To You

Through his transparency in the pages of this book, Tyrone Lister has provided a way for you to move pass the fears, phobias and obstacles that hold you captive and prohibit you from fully embracing life. *Getting Back To You* overflows with practical, applicable, hands-on tools that show you how to begin the journey to *Getting Back to You*! The practical wisdom that he has written is parallel to the system I used to get back to me. So, if you are ready, willing, anxious and eager to start your journey back to you, then Getting *Back to You* by Tyrone Lister is what you need to truly get back to the YOU that you know you can be!!

~Renee Hornbuckle, President/Founder
Renee Hornbuckle Ministries
www.reneehornbuckle.com

"Tyrone Lister gives us a blueprint and the tools for anyone to get back in control of their lives. There is no one who would not benefit from reading this powerful book and applies these practical principles that will result in an enriched life."

~Valerie Carrington, Engineer
Entrepreneur and Life Coach

Tyrone is always worth listening to. Having personally benefited in a life-changing way from this man's mentorship, I can recommend "Getting Back To You" enthusiastically. I can think of no one more qualified as a teacher, coach, guide and maximizer than Tyrone Lister giving practical insight on the priority, process and practice to refire your passion for living the best you!

~Dr. Kenneth D. Davis
Resident Pastor
The Wisdom Center
www.empowered2empower.com

This revelation and disclosing dissertation that my friend Tyrone Lister has pinned is both insightful and transparent, revealing the struggle of overcoming the grip of fear which is the mother of mental, emotional and spiritual penalization. He shares the procedures and processes that he employed to overcome and secure the victory over the grip of anxiety and panic. You will find that you are empowered to do the same.

~ Bishop Reginald D. Jordan
Founder & President
Inspiring Temple of Praise & Overseer of CIC
www.inspiringtemple.com

Tyrone Lister is one of the most Dynamic and Seasoned Speakers and Leaders of our time. He has been a coach and mentor to me helping me discover my true self. I highly recommend his latest masterpiece "Getting Back To You," to everyone who desires to conquer their fears, panic & anxiety to live a life of success.

~ Jesse Maranga
International Recording Artist
Entrepreneur

Going out on your own can be scary. But this book is a welcome antidote to that fear. It brims with savvy advice and nearly overflows with practical, hands-on exercises. Once you absorb the knowledge in these pages, you will be ready, willing, and eager to fashion a more rewarding life.

~James W. Phelps
Retired Military; Business Professional

It is my honor to endorse the man, Tyrone Lister; he has done a wonderful job in writing the book "Getting Back To You," out of his own struggles and life experiences. I believe the man is the book, and as another best-selling book says, "we are a living epistle written and read of all men." I recommend to all to get to know him by reading this motivational, transparent, and inspiring book. I am honored to call him my friend and I believe in Tyrone and am proud of the many that he has helped around the world by sharing his heart and story.

~Jamie Englehart
International Speaker Overseer of Heritage International Ministries

GETTING BACK◀◀ TO YOU

OVERCOME FEAR, PANIC, AND ANXIETY DISORDERS
THROUGH SPIRITUAL AND PSYCHOLOGICAL
CONDITONING TO ACCOMPLISH
A SUCCESSFUL LIFE!

TYRONE LISTER

GETTING BACK◄◄ TO YOU

OVERCOME FEAR, PANIC, AND ANXIETY DISORDERS
THROUGH SPIRITUAL AND PSYCHOLOGICAL
CONDITIONING TO ACCOMPLISH
A SUCCESSFUL LIFE!

TYRONE LISTER

Tyrone Lister

Getting Back To You
Copyright © 2012 by Tyrone Lister

Library of Congress Cataloging-in-Publication Data

1st ed.   p. cm.

ISBN 978-1479357413

Printed in the United States of America

Cover Designer: Daniel Marand, Platinum Services

Published by Jabez Books (A Division of Clark's Consultant Group): www.clarksconsultantgroup.com.

All rights reserved. No part of this publication may be reproduced, stored in a retrieval system, or transmitted in any form or by any means, electronic, mechanical, scanning, or otherwise, except as permitted under Section 107 or 108 of the 1976 United States Copyright Act, without either the prior written permission of the Publisher, or authorization through payment of the appropriate per-copy fee to the Copyright Clearance Center, Inc., 222 Rosewood Drive, Danvers, MA 01923. On the web at www.copyright.com.

1. Self – Development   2 Christianity – Spiritual
3. Confidence – Success

Limited Liabilities/Disclaimer of Warranty: While the publisher and author have used their best efforts in preparing this book, they make no representations or warranties with respect to the accuracy or completeness of the contents of this book and specifically disclaim any implied warranties of merchantability or fitness for a particular purpose. No warranty will be created or extended by sales representatives or written sales materials. The advice and strategies contained herein may not be suitable for your situation. The publisher is not engaged in rendering professional services, and you should consult with a professional where appropriate. Neither the publisher nor author shall be liable for any loss of profit or to her commercial damages, including but not limited to special, incidental, consequential, or other damages.

Getting back to YOU!

A journey to rediscovering the powerful, successful, and peaceful YOU!

DEDICATION

Motivation

I want to dedicate this book to my loving wife, Angelia Lister, who has been an inspiration to me through my transitions of life.

Inspiration

Also, I dedicate this book to my son, Zion Samuel Lister, who is a bright shining star in my life. I love you to life!

Celebration

In loving memory of my grandmother, Irene Burks, who I lovingly call, "Big Mama." She taught me how to be strong, how to survive and, how to bounce back from any situation that life may bring.

TABLE OF CONTENTS

The Real Deal ……………………………..23

A Day I Will Never Forget…………………….30

CHAPTER 1

Making A Comback……………………………35

      The Reason for It All

A Long Way From Home…………………….42

CHAPTER 2

CONSECRATION..................................47
The Preparation For Change

Focus...56

Master Your Emotions................................59

Get A Grip!...62

Change Your Reality Perception 64

Create Your Desired Outcome................66

CHAPTER 3

INFORMATION..................................69
The Instruction For Change

The Structure Of The Mind......................73

A New Core..79

CHAPTER 4

SATURATION............................…..83

The Fuel For Change

Visualization………………………………..88

Meditation…………………………………….93

Becoming One With Your Vision…………96

Continuation…………………………………..99

CHAPTER 5

DELIBERATION……………………………..103

The Plan For Change

Mental Energy……………………………..107

Persuasion……………………………………..110

On Purpose Intent………………………….112

Action Plan..................................114

Preparing a Plan..........................115

A Word to the Wise......................119

CHAPTER 6

DETERMINATION…………………….……..121
The Discipline For Change

Building Life With the Storm In Mind...124

Why…………………………………………….129

The Breaking Point………………………136

CHAPTER 7

EXPECTATION.........................**139**

The Belief In Change

Proven Principles That Work..............145

The Future Now Showing...................147

Believe...151

CHAPTER 8

MANIFESTATION...............................**155**

The Result Of Change

Pleasure Out Of Pain...........................160

Through The Valley..............................163

I Did It...167

CHAPTER 9

CELEBRATION....................**169**
The Accomplishment Of Change

Party Time.................................173

You..175

Pay It Forward..........................178

CHAPTER 10

AFTERWARDS......................**181**
What's Really Happening?

Guild and Embarrassment................184

Partners....................................186

Let It Go...................................189

CONCLUSION.............................**193**
Final Thoughts

THE REAL DEAL

The State of Flux

Flux is a state of uncertainty about what should be done (usually following some important event) preceding the establishment of a new direction or action.

Life is filled with uncertainties on many levels. Uncertainties that can have the power to cause us to doubt, experience fear, and have anxiety about our future. If someone had told me 20 years ago that I would have to champion issues, like the ones I am getting ready to share with you in this book, along with paralyzing and life stopping panic attacks, I would have said, you don't know what you are talking about!

I grew up in a small town in Texas named Corsicana. I was raised by my grandmother for the majority of my childhood. I was her only and favorite grandson. She was a business owner, and as a result of that, I learned how to think like a business owner. I learned how to be confident, strong as well as how to work with people.

I was a product of a divorced home. My parents divorced when I was two years old. About twice a month I would go visit my mother and once every three months visit my father. This created a continual state of emotional flux when I would return to my grandmother's.

This went on for years, but it was not until I was in the sixth grade that its affect on my life show up. There was such a build up from this emotional flux in my psyche that as a young man at the beginning stages of adolescence, I didn't know if I was going to be a child one day or an adult the next day. There were all kinds of emotional changes I experienced. I remember I spent the majority of my sixth grade year emotionally depressed. Whenever I visited my parents and they dropped me off at my grandmother's home, I would cry for three days afterwards. This uncontrollable emotional state gripped me so strong that I could not focus on my schoolwork; therefore, I ended up failing the sixth grade.

At age 13, I moved out of town with my mother. I thought I was ready for this change, but somehow the pain of leaving my grandmother, my friends and my surroundings overshadowed the joy of living with my mother. I was suddenly in a new house, in a new bed, in a new school, with new people and everything was different. After a while I learned how to adjust and move on and to make the best of it, because my grandmother taught me to be strong and how to champion life regardless of what challenges I may experience.

As an adult, I became the problem solver and peacekeeper in our family. I found myself functioning in these roles so much with my family that eventually, I developed a *"get over it and move on"* attitude. I had become very callous to my own emotions. I was being strong as I had been taught.

Two years after my wife and I were married, and she was pregnant with our first and only child, we decided to move both of my parents into our home to live with us. This was no small task because my parents were divorced for almost 30 years and were both very independent. Much to my surprised, they both agreed and a new dimension of life began.

At that time my mother had survived cancer for 18 years, and my father at 79 was in perfect health. With much joy and anticipation our first son was born! We were so excited. During that time my mother's health started to fail quickly.

She was in and out of the hospital for weeks at a time.

Around that same time my father, who had been retired for several years, received notice that he would no longer be eligible for retirement compensation. Because of the stress of this situation, he had a stroke. He was immediately hospitalized and was there for 30 days. At the same time my mother was admitted into the same hospital for several weeks because of her health.

Everyday my wife and I including our new son spent hours at the hospital. My father never recovered from his stroke and passed in the hospital. Eight months later my mother was on life support, and to my dismay, I alone had to make the decision to pull the plug.

I performed the eulogies of both of my parents and for me, as a sign of resolve; I closed both of their caskets. This was a major state of flux for me and my family.

But we grieved, moved on, and started a whole new chapter of life.

Three years later, I was leading a group of people on a consistent basis that brought with it its own set of challenges. Not only was I making decisions that affected me and my family's life, I was now making decisions that affected the people's lives in this group on many different levels. Anyone who is a leader and has to make these types of decisions understands that sometimes the people you lead might like your decisions and sometimes they do not. Because of this, I was experiencing very high levels of stress.

A Day I Will Never Forget

The Saturday before Mother's Day was peaceful. I was shopping for my wife and spent most of the day alone. Later that evening, she joined me for dinner. When we returned home, I went to my home office to catch up on some work for the week. As I sat at my desk, I started feeling weird. I had shortness of breath and was literally hyperventilating. I walked out of my office in hopes that I could get a grip on things. Everything I did made the situation worse. My left arm down to my fingers was tingling. I felt faint and disoriented. I literally thought I was dying. Finally, I was able to calm down and eventually go to sleep.

The next day I had to speak at a Mother's Day event. I was able to accomplish this task with confidence, but when I left the platform those feelings came again. The next day I went to the urgent care center, told them about my symptoms, and they prescribed some medicine to help calm me. When I took the medicine, it did help me sleep, but when I woke up the same symptoms were there again.

I was unable to travel. I was unable to eat at restaurants. I was afraid to be alone. I stayed awake all night from the fear of dying in my sleep. This literally confined me to my house. I lost about 20 pounds (that's a lot for me), and little did I know that this would change the quality of my way of life for the next six months.

About 30 days after these symptoms continued, I decided to go see my family doctor. I told her what was going on, and that now I have physical pain in my body that was unbearable. After a few more questions about the symptoms, she asked me what I enjoyed doing. After my answer, she left her office and returned with a prescription for rest and relaxation with no medication. She told me that I had anxiety disorders and my situation was caused by years and layers of stress that was never dealt with or resolved, and the best thing for me to do was to learn how to **get back to you!**

Over the next five months, I made a quality decision that I was going to champion this situation instead of it championing me. During this time, I created a system that helped me recondition my mind and to press the reset button in my life. My desire, drive and determination for a better life helped me stick to my resolve. Through the methods that I am sharing in this book, I was able to find the path to get back to me. And I am confident that if you are experiencing some of the same disorders that I experienced, you will find the path to GET BACK TO **YOU** after reading this book!

In these pages, I will show you proven methods to help you identify and overcome fear, panic and anxiety disorders, through spiritual and psychological conditioning to accomplish a successful life!

Chapter One

MAKING A COMEBACK

The Reason For It All

A **comeback** is a spiritual and psychological process of being restored back to or beyond a previous position, posture or privilege lost or stolen due to adversity.

There are five major components to your soul: your mind, will, imagination, emotions, and your intellect. When these five parts are working together in harmony, you are able to achieve a balance in your soul. This balance is what produces peace and helps you move through life and achieve the highest level of success in any area. Life has a unique way of allowing us to experience situations and issues that fragment our soul and throw us off balance. Because of this imbalance, we can lose time, energy, and life that often leaves us splintered and detached.

This disconnection from the lack of emotional and mental resolve is what opens us up to the affects of fear, panic and anxiety.

There is a story of a young son that asked his father for his inheritance. Even though his father was reluctant to give him his inheritance, he gave it to him anyway. And the young man after receiving his inheritance, left home. Because of the son's lack of maturity, he spent all of his money unwisely even to the point that he had no money for food. Therefore, he became so distraught that he found himself in a pig's pin. As he searched vigorously for food, all he found was corn husks. But he was in such a famish state that he decided to eat it regardless. However, this story shares something interesting. It says right before he ate the husk that *he came to himself.*

This has always been an interesting story to me because it is so amazing how you can come to yourself. My question was always, where did he go from himself?

After I experienced the paralyzing grip of fear, panic and anxiety, which I call the big three (3), I learned how a person could actually go away from himself. This is not a physical action, but more of a spiritual and psychological response.

There is usually some type of adversity that causes us to experience this exit from a normal healthy and happy life. Through my ordeal, I was able to experience (all that I went through with my parents and the people I was leading) this first hand.

As I was finding my way back to myself, I found out generally there were four reasons that we experience this hardship that gets our lives off track. Here is the list and their definitions:

1. **Fears**: When dread grips you and alters your life's activities.

2. **Frustrations**: An overwhelming sense of being annoyed especially if you have an inability to change or achieve something.

3. **Falsehoods**: Being presented a lie or feeling deceived.

4. **Fatigue**: Mental and Physical exhaustion.

GETTING BACK TO YOU COACHING TIP

> The road to "Getting Back To You" starts with a decision to get back to you.

These are many things that can impair or impede our ability to maintain balance and wholeness in any stage of life. So regardless of the path that led you to your current state, whatever it might be (fearful, unsure of yourself or perhaps, like this young man that life has led you to a pig's pen), I want you to know that there is still hope and there is a way out of your mess.

A Long Way From Home

Maybe you have heard the saying "home is where the heart is." But if not, it is an expression that refers to a special place where we feel safe from harm, securely locked away from danger.

For many people home has a different meaning. For some, it is a four bedroom house in a suburban neighborhood. For others, it is an apartment in the inner city. Yet for some, it is a mobile home in a trailer park. Sadly for others, it is a cardboard box on the street. Whatever home may be to you, it is that place where you arrive to (regardless of the situation(s) that facilitated the process), you know in your heart that you are home.

The first step in getting back to you and finding your way back home is deciding that you have had enough and you are ready to get back to your spiritual and psychological place of balance that I call "home".

The story about the son in the pig's pin continues after he came to himself. It goes on to say how the son thought about his family situation and upbringing, that even the servants in his father's house ate well and had leftovers. Then the young man figured that he could go back home and be a servant in his father's house, and at least eat well. And there on that day in that pig's pin, he made a decision that he had enough and wanted to change his life and go back home.

Putting aside any fears that he had about how he would be received when he returned home, he started his journey back home (to himself).

His initial plan was to enter the servant's quarters and try to fit in from there. But while he was a good distance away his father saw him, ran to him and hugged him. Then afterward, he put a ring on his finger, welcomed him home and had a celebration in his honor. The father was happy because his son that was lost and estranged had come back home.

Perhaps, right now, you can identify with this story. You are a long way from home or a long way from your "authentic" self. Just like this son, you have the innate ability to return home and come back to yourself.

It all starts with a decision. Much like this young man, you will find that the response to your return will be much better than you could have ever imagined.

Are you ready to get started? Are you ready to get back to you? Are you ready to return home? If so, take this journey with me as we begin the first step to your recovery process. It's an experience of a lifetime and I am excited that I can help guide you through the getting back to you process. Let's start the journey.

Chapter Two

CONSECRATION

The Preparation For Change

Consecration means to dedicate solemnly to a service or goal.

I remember when I was starting one of my businesses; I was excited and after careful calculation jumped in with both feet. After the first day of working, it hit me; I have got to wrap my mind around what I just started.

To do this, I had to consecrate myself to the purpose. So I took about a week and during this time, I was thinking, planning, and casting vision for what I wanted to accomplish. I had to do some "soul searching" as the old cliché goes, and really devote myself to this purpose. This was going to require time, energy, and focused effort in addition to what I was already doing. So during my consecration time, I was preparing for change.

GETTING BACK TO YOU COACHING TIP

Deep inside, you must have the desire to change

I believe we all have dreams and want to live better lives. And somewhere deep within, we have the desire to make it happen. We want the end result to be the dream that we see on the canvas of our imagination. What makes it difficult and seemingly sometimes impossible is the fact that you want to live a better life, but you are consumed with emotions such as fear and anxiety. And if you have ever faced any of the paralyzing conditions that come along with these abnormalities, you fully understand.

When you make the decision to go forward, one of the main things you will have to do is get clarity. Clarification will help you make sense of it all. It puts the pieces together, and most importantly, it helps you discover why?

When you discover the reason that you are making these changes, it starts the wheel of passion moving in you. Your why could be to increase the quality of your life or to help you move toward your dream. Your why could also be that you don't want to pass this on to your children or your why could simply be, you don't want to live like this anymore.

When you discover your why, it is your greater reason for living and the fuel to help you accomplish your goals and reach your dreams in life. In chapter three, I will talk more about how to develop your why, but right now let me get back to the consecration stage.

Your consecration time could be a day, a week, a month or however long it takes you to prepare yourself for what you are getting ready to do. When you are setting yourself aside for your purpose, you want to ask the "who, what, when, where, and why" questions. It is important during this time to get as much clarity as possible.

You want to pull out your likes and dislikes -- what makes you happy, what motivates you, and what inspires you. This is the time to discover and really get acquainted with the authentic you. For example, some of the things that inspire me are light, sound, and movement. I also like to be in wide open spaces with windows to look outside.

So once I was clear on what I wanted, I was able to draw these things into my atmosphere that helped me create a positive mental attitude. Your atmosphere will affect what you expect and what you receive according to Dr. I.V Hilliard, CEO of New Light in Houston, TX.

Okay, here's what I want you to do now. Get a journal or something you can write in, turn to the first blank sheet of paper and at the top write "getting back to you." On the first line write the question what do I really want?

Please take some time to search yourself and decide what you really want. List five to ten things. Go over your list again and make sure these are the things you really want to accomplish. This is a very critical step in you achieving your desired outcome. If you don't have a journal you can start here.

_____

_____

_____

_____

_____

_____

_____

It is said that a goal is not a goal until you make it public. Writing these things down will be your personal way of making it public. With this list, you have now started a desire and pathway for you to get back to YOU.

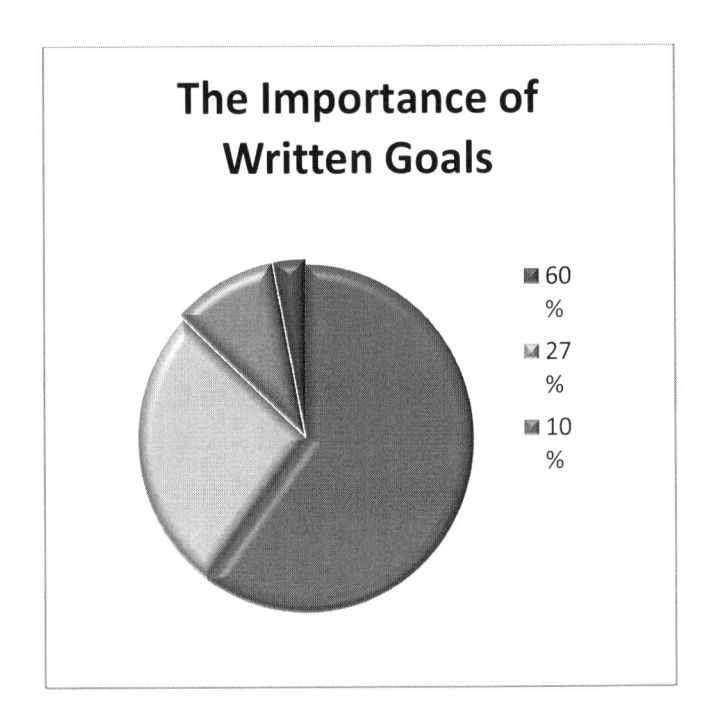

The Importance of Written Goals

- 60%
- 27%
- 10%

- 3% have a written, specific goal for change
- 10% have a general goal and make comfortable change
- 27% have no goals and experience minimal to no change
- 60% have survival habits and locked in a stall position

Focus

One of the greatest problems that we face as individuals is broken focus. Small gradual and deceptive changes over a period of time can cause you to drift off course, and before you know it, you end up some place that you are not familiar with and have no idea how you got there.

Two of the major steps in any refocusing plan are:

(1) Recognition

(2) Admittance

When you recognize that you have missed your goal or you have slipped out of sync with your vision, and you are not where you want to be, it can cause frustration, anger and resentment along with many other negative emotions. So it would be to your advantage to recognize where you are quickly, so that you can move forward in the getting back to YOU process.

The next step in the recovery of your focus is to admit. This is sometimes the most difficult step in the whole process.

People generally respond in three ways #1 denial (this is not true); #2 illusion (your created reality); or #3 blame (it was someone or something's fault) according to the book *Emotional BS* by Dr. Carl Alasko.

To admit means you take 100% of the responsibility for the decisions that you have made and accept the challenge to change. This is where focus will begin. If you want to change, you must do things differently. It is said the definition of insanity is doing the same things repeatedly and expecting different results.

I understand that there are life situations that can get you off focus -- an unexpected death, health issues, family crises, change in employment or deployment. All of these detractors can alters your path and impair your focus. All of these situations are a real and valid part of life. The decisions that you make during and after these events will determine the quality of life you will experience in your future. If you start a line that you are walking called focus that leads you to your destination, you have to be committed enough to the process to stay on the line when life happens.

Master Your Emotions.

One of the components of the soul is your emotions. There are many definitions that define your emotions, but here is the working definition that we are going to use for this book. **Emotions** are the various bodily feelings associated with mood, temperament, personality, disposition, and motivation. Here are some of the major emotions: happy, excited, tender, sad, angry, and scared. Our emotions are generally in a state of flux (continual change). If we allow them, our emotions will have us on the proverbial rollercoaster. Up and down every few seconds. This is why it is important to control your emotions instead of your emotions controlling you.

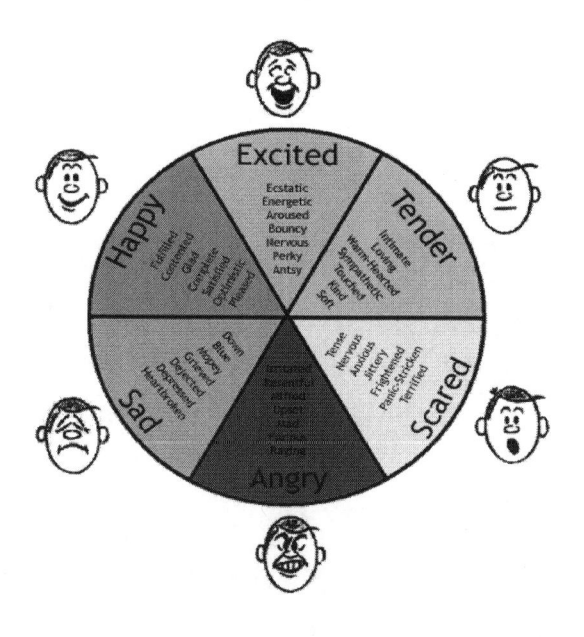

Wikipedia.com

Your emotional state affects your perception and outlook about every situation. This is key in learning how to get back to YOU, especially if you experience fear, anxiety and/or panic.

Here are some of the basic ways that you can start the process of controlling your emotions.

GETTING BACK TO YOU
COACHING TIP

> Your emotional state affects
> your perception and outlook about
> every situation.

Get A Grip!

When you start feeling the familiar feeling that sparks your emotional cycle, do something that breaks your thought pattern. Shake yourself, yell, tug your ear, talk to yourself or find someone to talk to. Whatever you do know that it is to help you get a grip and change your thought pattern. The longer you follow a disempowering thought process; it will cause your current emotional state to increase.

When I experienced these feelings and emotional imbalance, I trained my subconscious mind to respond in a positive and constructive way. For example, when I would feel the sense of overwhelm or wanting to panic. The first thing I would do was shift my eyes back and forth and start talking to myself saying, "You know what this is, get a grip, this is a temporary occurrence, and not reality."

I know it may sound weird to talk to yourself, but if it works, you may want to consider it. In fact, more and more professionals in the mental health arena have found that self-talk is really a healthy practice when speaking positive affirmations. The key here is to break the disempowering thought cycle, so that you can avert the possibility of a full panic or anxiety attack in order to regain control.

GETTING BACK TO YOU COACHING TIP

> Your emotions are connected to your belief system

Change Your Reality Perception

After you get a grip, the next step is to create an empowering thought pattern that helps you view the current reality as it is. Let me give you an example. The first time that I experienced overwhelming anxiety and uncontrollable panic, I was flying to Las Vegas. I had no idea what was happening, but I knew that I did not like it. I got up from my seat, walked around, and started talking to anyone who would listen. In my mind, I told myself, "The plane will land soon." So I sat back down and went to sleep until the plane landed.

Because of that experience whenever I would get on a plane, I would sense this overwhelming feeling again and again. So now when I fly, I change my reality perception, and I tell myself through positive confessions that this is going to be a great flight. I will sit next to someone that I like. I will not experience panic or anxiety, and I may add a few more things depending on my current emotional state. What I am doing is changing my perception from fear and worry to excitement and expectation.

Create Your Desired Outcome

How do you want to live? What type of life do you desire? Think about the quality of life you want. If you want a life free from fear, panic or anxiety, then I want you to visualize yourself living life at that level. For example, if you experience social anxiety disorder (fear of crowds), I want you to see yourself on the canvas of your imagination in a crowd, laughing and talking, really enjoying yourself. Think about how you would feel. What would the room look like? Who do you want to be in the crowd? Be as detailed as you can.

GETTING BACK TO YOU COACHING TIP

The longer you follow a disempowering thought process; it will cause your current emotional stage to increase.

With this vision and thought, I want you to focus on how you feel and the response that you give to the crowd. Think about how the crowd will respond to you. This is a part of what is called, "mind conditioning." It is important for you to create your desired outcome. How you create and maintain your PMA (positive mental attitude) will determine what you experience in life. The ancient proverb says, "As a man thinks in his heart so is he." This is true. You are the only person that can change your perception and create the results that you desire in your life.

Chapter Three

INFORMATION

The Instruction For Change

The power to change is locked inside your ability to receive, process, and to follow the instructions that you are exposed to. In this chapter we will look at the concept of how the mind processes, stores and retrieves information from a psychological perspective. I am not a psychiatrist; however, the information that I discovered in my research may prove helpful to you.

There is a slogan that says, "A mind is a terrible thing to waste." I agree wholeheartedly with this, especially if the mind has fallen prey to fear, anxiety, and panic. These crippling disorders will grip your soul and paralyze you from living life to its highest level.

It is said that the instruction that you follow is the instruction that will increase in your life. If you follow positive and healthy instructions, you will get a favorable outcome. If you follow negative and destructive instructions, you will get an unfavorable outcome. It is all in the instructions YOU follow.

GETTING BACK TO YOU COACHING TIP

The Getting Back to You Process is sustained by right information.

A key element of change is how we respond to new instructions and how we allow new information to flow into our minds. The goal is to replace the old disempowering mindsets with a positive result-based mindset. Let's take a journey and discover some information that will be the foundation and instructions for the change you desire.

The Structure of the Mind

There are three components of the mind:

1. The Conscious mind
2. The Subconscious mind
3. The Conscience mind

These three work together in a dynamic systematic way as our onboard computer to keep our lives on course.

- **The Conscious mind**

The *Conscious mind* is in charge of the purposeful and intentional day to day conscious thoughts and decisions. The initial logical thinking and reasoning that are required for concentration and where purposeful thinking is handled.

- **The Subconscious mind**

The *Subconscious mind* is the programmed hard drive of the

conscious mind. Its purpose is to carry out the instructions that were given by the conscious mind.

After the conscious mind has processed through certain information and accepted certain norms and values as truth, from that moment on, the subconscious starts to make decisions on a level that does not require much conscious effort at all.

Here is how this works. Think of the time when you first learned how to ride a bicycle. The beginning was a little uncertain and it required a lot of conscious effort. During the learning experience, your hands gripped the handle bars tightly and your palms were sweating. You were engaged on many levels. You may have even fallen a couple of times. But after a while, riding a bicycle became an automatic experience that required little conscious effort.

Now, even after several years, you still know the basics of riding a bicycle. The reason you are able to do this is because your subconscious mind was designed to help you carry out task that have been intentionally learned. The subconscious mind serves the conscious mind and eliminates the necessity to rethink known information over and over again.

- **The Conscience mind**

The **Conscience mind** is where your belief and value systems are housed. Your conscience is the foundation of your belief system, your reference point by which all things are judged. It is here that there is a preset standard that all things are judged by.

As you experience life and decide to believe and value certain things, your standard of judgment is developed and your conscience **now** acts as your central processing center. After information is processed through the conscious mind and received as truth in the subconscious mind the communication between the subconscious mind and the conscience mind is automatic. This communication is done on an ongoing basis without much thought. The information stored here is the guiding structure of your life and where everything that you perceive as true or false comes from.

The conscious mind is like the processor. The subconscious mind is like the hard drive and the conscience mind is the foundation that all mental activity is built on.

GETTING BACK TO YOU COACHING TIP

Your thoughts and actions control where you are going in life.

A New Core

Fear, panic and anxiety disorders are all conditions of the mind. They are all expressed through your soul (mind, will, imagination, emotions, and intellect). The goal is to recognize what produces these overwhelming sensations that have very real implications. Here are a couple of examples: when you are in an elevator and you feel claustrophobic because you are alone and you have a fear that it will get stuck and you won't have a phone signal to call anyone for help. Or maybe you are deathly afraid of heights and the higher the elevator goes the more fearful you become. Whatever the case may be, it is important to know that this is an expression of fear that acts like a trip wire that activates different emotional expressions and produces very real side effects.

When you recognize the basis of where these emotional expressions come from, then you are able to start creating a foundation to build the platform for the change that you desire in your life. This is the place where you can begin to create a new core. Your core is your subconscious mind or as stated earlier, your hard drive where information has been stored and perceived as truth about any situation. It is information that you receive through words that are spoken, images that you see, and experiences that you have had, which all shape your core to respond positively or negatively to any situation.

So to create a new core you have to receive new information that process through your conscious mind enough times that it causes your subconscious mind to recognize this information as truth to erase the previous information and replace it with the new. One of the basic ways to learn is through repetition. If you repeat a practice enough times it becomes a habit. This process is how you change your subconscious mind and get it to receive new information as truth.

The first two months of my experience with panic attacks everything seemed so unreal. I was dealing with the idea that I could possibly be this way for the rest of my life. I thought about never being able to travel again or go to a restaurant or do any of the things that I enjoyed because of fear. But somewhere deep inside me, I thought that if I could get someone to talk to me in a positive manner that I could somehow get back on track.

From that small knowing inside of me somewhere, I started searching for material that would help me be positive. I knew that I needed someone to coach me, so I went to the bookstore and bought an audio book by Norman Vincent Peale called *"The Power of Positive Thinking."* I listened to this book daily -- over and over again.

Eventually, within a short time, I noticed I began to feel a little better, so I surrounded myself with other positive resources that dealt with my thinking and my spiritual walk. I also bought a CD from one of my mentors, where she would repeat positive confessions. And again, repeatedly, I would listen and read this information, while taking notes of what I learned and felt. At that time, little did I know, I was literally changing my core and creating the type of positive outcome that I so desperately desired.

Chapter Four

SATURATION

The Fuel For Change

I was speaking at a seminar designed specifically for men and one of the men asked me a question about how to deal with ongoing anger in a specific area of his life. He said that this anger intensified when he would do positive things to get rid of it, and he wanted to know why this happened and what he needed to do to change it. I gave him this illustration.

If you have a clear glass that represents you, and fill it with dirt one-fourth (¼) of the way that represents your anger; like the dirt, your emotion will settle, and eventually you will become comfortable with its response. Then I told him to fill the glass with water that represents positive inputs. When you pour more water or positive inputs into a negative situation it raises the negative to the top. While it is rising, you feel the effects of those emotions moving through you and many times intensifies beyond the initial feeling. I told him the key was to saturate the glass with water until the dirt overflowed and was no longer a part of the glass.

This is how saturation works. The more of the positive input that you take in the more you have a reference and belief that you can change. Remember positive inputs can be speaking, listening, and experiencing positive atmospheres. We are all affected by our five senses (touch, feel, taste, smell, and sound). This is why it is important to create the type of atmosphere that will motivate you to be positive. With your surroundings and your on purpose intent, you can saturate your subconscious mind and literally force it to recognize new information as truth. Now, let's walk through this process.

GETTING BACK TO YOU
COACHING TIP

Your positive inputs must outweigh your negative inputs to create the results that you desire

Visualization

A vision in its most simple form is a picture of a preferred future or desired outcome. For example, maybe you have seen on the canvas of your imagination having more than enough money to live comfortable, give to your favorite charities, and yet have much more left over. Maybe you see yourself in shape and healthy. Or maybe you see yourself flying across the Grand Canyon in a helicopter, vacationing in some exotic place, having a better marriage, or just being free from anxiety and panic. Whatever your vision is, it is a preferred future or a desired outcome.

This is where you create your **WHY**. Your why is the reason that you want to be free from fear, panic, and anxiety. It is what pushes you to put in the work to get the results you desire. Your why is what motivates you and speaks to you when you want to quit. Your why is deep in you and has been calling out to you all along. Your why has to be big enough to push you to go after it. It is said that if your why doesn't make you cry, then it's not big enough. Right now, I want you to answer these questions. The answer to these questions will be a clue to your why.

1. What makes me cry? This is a clue to what you are supposed to *heal*.

_____

_____

_____

_____

_____

_____

2. What makes me angry? This is a clue to what you are supposed to *fix*.

_____
_____
_____
_____
_____
_____

3. What makes me happy? This is a clue to what you are supposed to *enjoy*.

_____
_____
_____
_____
_____
_____

When you recognize a greater purpose for living, it helps you move pass any barriers obstructing your vision and path, and it will propel you to start *living* instead of just *existing*. There are some that may already know what their why is; but perhaps, you have lost it. All you have to do is repaint the picture on the canvas of your imagination and go for it!

A vision without a plan is just a nightmare.
~Unknown Author

The first thing you have to do is solidify in your mind that you are greater than what you have become. You were created for something better than fear. You are bigger than these panic attacks. It all begins with a positive thought and a vision of something better. When your conscious mind captures a vision, it then communicates it to your subconscious mind and when your subconscious mind receives it as truth, it automatically and immediately creates ways for you to accomplish this vision. Have you ever seen a car that you really liked and wanted to own it? And shortly after, it seems like you would see that particular car everywhere. That is what the subconscious does -- it makes you more aware of what is available and creates ways to accomplish what you see.

Meditation

Your mind is your instrument. Learn to be its master and not its slave.

~Unknown Author

Meditation is a spiritual experience that produces a change in your mental complex operation and can permanently affect your decision making process. The definition of meditation means to mutter, to put to work, to muse over, to practice beforehand, and to actualize what is in your spiritual world. Therefore, Meditation is an ancient biblical method for accelerating the transformation of the conscious mind because it speaks the language of the subconscious mind and the conscious mind.

GETTING BACK TO YOU COACHING TIP

What you meditate on the most will determine what you expect and what you experience during your Getting Back to YOU Process.

I was first exposed to this concept in the latter 90s when I read a book by Dr. I.V. Hilliard titled, <u>Mental Toughness for Success</u>. Through study, experience and spiritual knowledge, I have come to understand how to apply these concepts to improve the quality of my life and be free from the paralyzing grip of fear, panic, and anxiety. Because of this, I have helped thousands of lives around the world.

Meditation is what has enhanced my spirituality and is the basis for any true change that I have experienced in my life. Whether it was being free from a horrible lifestyle of fear, panic, and anxiety or getting my desired outcome in any situation.

Becoming One With Your Vision

This practice helps take your vision, which is your preferred future or desired outcome, and create the framework to make it a reality. You are now taking your thoughts' concepts and ideas into your subconscious mind and downloading germinated information onto your mind's hard drive. This process also involves your soul (your mind, will, imagination, emotions and your intellect). During the meditation process, you may take a positive confession about yourself and speak it out loud repeatedly, then be silent and focus your mind on your desired outcome seeing yourself actually experiencing it. This is the beginning of how you create lasting change.

GETTING BACK TO YOU COACHING TIP

> When you believe you can, your posture will change

Also, your physiological state will help assist you in the meditation process. The physiological state is your literal behavior, posture, actions, and mindset that you adjust while meditating. For example, if your are meditating on being confident while meeting new people, your physiological state can assist you by relaxing your shoulders, straightening your back and imagining yourself looking someone in the eye and giving them a firm handshake. It is the posture that you take while meditating on your desired outcome. This is more than memorizing your positive confession. This is actually being there in your mind and soul. At this point, the mind can't tell what is real or what is not.

For example, have you ever had a dream of something frightful or exhilarating and when you woke up during the dream you were breathing hard, sweating profusely, and your heart was beating fast? What was happening? Your mind was not able to tell the difference from a dream or reality. This is an example of how you train your mind to accept a new reality.

Now you are becoming one with your confession, which is the pathway of transforming you from who you are to who you desire to be.

Continuation

One of the major components of success is continuing and completing what you start. On the journey back to YOU, you will encounter the desire to give up and revert back to what is familiar. So as you start the change process to be free from fear, panic and anxiety, you have to make the predetermined decision that you are not going to give up. You will not throw in the towel, and you will not surrender to a paralyzing lifestyle.

GETTING BACK TO YOU COACHING TIP

Create habits of success that mirror your goals and objectives in life!

As we conclude this chapter, it is important that you understand that repetition forms your mindset, which is a powerful tools to help you learn as well as aide in the saturation process. An action repeated long enough becomes a habit. My goal with this book is to help you create the habit of success!

Chapter Five

DELIBERATION

The Plan For Change

Victoria was a woman who had a physical ailment for 12 years. She went from doctor to doctor, but neither of them was able to find a cure for her. Therefore, after hearing no after no for many years, her self-esteem was low. In addition, she was physically and financially drained. But one day she heard that there was someone in town that could possibly help her with her condition. Even though she was exhausted and emotional drained, she wanted to be free from her condition so bad that somehow she found the strength and courage to seek help again.

She dressed and left her home with the intention and purpose to find this person. She found the person, but he was surrounded by a crowd of people, which thwarted her from getting to him. At that moment she made a life-changing decision. Victoria decided that she had suffered long enough and she was not going to give up now! She pushed her way through the crowd and after much resistance, she got to him. Her purposeful pursuit paid off. Not only did he give her a cure for her condition, he gave her a plan to recover all that she lost during her 12 year journey.

Victoria's encounter with this man changed her life forever because she made a deliberate decision about changing her situation. As a result, she was cured. If you would activate "deliberation" in your life, you will see the results that you desire as well.

Mental Energy

In Physics we learn that energy is neither created nor destroyed, but it can be transferred. Energy is defined as power which may be translated into motion, overcoming resistance, or effecting physical change; the ability to do work. It is important that during the deliberation process that you learn how to transfer the energy in your body to your mind, so that you can fully overcome any resistance to your getting back to YOU process. Mental energy is what assists you in creating a good mental flow of positive thoughts as well as aides in boosting your confidence to accomplish your task. On the next page, there is a chart that will show you a few ways that you can create a good mental energy flow.

Mental Energy

TOO MUCH	TOO LITTLE
Excessive Worrying	Mentally Flat
Negative Thinking	Drifting Thoughts
Racing Thoughts	Don't Care Attitude
Inability to Concentrate	Unmotivated

What to do to change

Remember Past Success	Focus On One Step At A Time
Focus On One Step At A Time	Set Challenging Goals
Shift Your Focus	Visualize Your Desired Goal
Positive Self-Talk	Positive Self Talk

The subject of mental energy is much greater that what I have shared with you in this book, but it is a place for you to get started.

Now that you have the concept of mental energy, you can use this theory throughout your entire getting back to YOU process.

Persuasion

In my study of people over the last two and a half decades, I have found that persuasion is one of the most powerful tools in conditioning your mind to overcome fear, panic, and anxiety. I define persuasion as change based on influence and evidence. There are three categories of persuasion that I have found to be the dominate ways that people respond to change.

1. **Passive Conclusive** – This is when a person has been introduced to new information and it influences them enough to try this new concept because it seems good.

2. **Present Consent** – In this stage persuasion is based on the current information that moves a person to believe. This stage involves a lot of emotional energy that influences a person's decisions.

3. **Persuaded Conviction** – During this stage a person has enough information that has influenced them to make a committed decision based on their beliefs and their desired end result. In this stage a person has developed a resolve that cannot be shaken.

Depending on what stage of persuasion you are at will determine how quickly you will move through your getting back to YOU process. My question is how bad do you want it? Are you willing to cope with the affects of fear, panic, and anxiety for the rest of your life? Or are you ready to make a change and live a successful life free from the big three? Your answer to these questions will determine your outcome to your situation. I hope that you are ready to make a change. Let's continue.

On Purpose Intent

Again, it is said that a goal is not a goal until you make it public. It's easy to say to yourself what you are going to do, but without accountability, it is easy to let yourself out of the deal because no one else will know. One of the most important steps in setting a goal is making a decision. Everything hinges on the decision that you make. Tony Robbins, a well-renowned 21st century motivational speaker, says, "Decide what you want and take massive actions to make it happen." Your massive actions have to have a massive plan so that you have a target and goal in mind. After you have put together a plan and made your decision to change your life, then you must have an on purpose intention, meaning having the mindset that "I AM" going to do this. An on purpose intent means that you have a resolve that cannot be shaken.

Action Plan

My concept of creating a plan is starting with the end in mind. Where do you want to be or what do you want to accomplish at the end of your plan? The next concept is what I call LTD -- Learnable Teachable and Doable.

So creating a plan you start with the end in mind and back up, breaking the process down into small simple steps. Let me show you how this works.

Example: Someone dealing with claustrophobia (an abnormal and persistent fear of closed spaces, or being closed in or being shut in, as in elevators, tunnels, or any other confined space).

Preparing a Plan

Goal: Ride elevators without fear of being closed in.

Let's say for example that you do better on an elevator that has a glass window so that you can see out.

1. Get a partner who can help you with this process and find a glass elevator so you can see outside and ride the elevator up and down as many times as you can. After the exercise breathe deep, exhale and relax.

2. Ride the same elevator up and down as many times as you can without your partner. After the exercise breathe deep, exhale and relax. (You decide the time intervals between exercises).

3. Step three is to repeat step one, but this time in a closed elevator. Make sure that you are going as high as you can. After the exercise breathe deep, exhale and relax.

4. Find an elevator and have your partner to stay outside of the building and ride the elevator up and down as many times as possible stopping on multiple floors where people are getting on and off. After the exercise breathe deep, exhale and relax.

5. Leave your partner at home and ride the elevator up and down several times until you create a new habit in your subconscious mind of peace and not fear about the elevator. After the exercise breathe deep, exhale and relax.

You will probably feel uncomfortable at first, but that is a part of the process. At the end of your exercise, exhale, breathe deep and relax.

There are several things that are important to any change process, but one of the most essential steps is how you prepare your mind going into the exercise.

Now, if you are planning at this point to venture out and face your "challenge" head on, don't forget to follow the steps in the previous chapter to help you condition your mind for each task. Then the next important step is your breathing pattern. Deep long breaths, inhaling in your nose and exhaling out of your mouth are what help regulate your body's response to panic and anxiety. I like to think of it as breathing in confidence and breathing out fear.

This is just an example of how to create an action plan. Some may have a more detailed plan, while others may have more or less steps. It all depends on the person and the situation. For more information on how to create an action plan for change go to www.tyronelister.com.

A Word to the Wise

Committing your goals to paper increases the liklihood of you achieving them 1,000 percent!

~Brian Tracy

After you have put some thought into your life's plan for change, the next step is to write it down. There is an old saying that says, "Don't just think it, ink it." I know that we have different types of technology available to us today from Ipads to voice recorders. The purpose here is to get it out of your mind and into a written format. This will help you visualize where you desire to go and it will also assist you in staying on track.

My friend Gary Eby says that "change is a door that you open from the inside." When you are ready to make a change and do something about your paralyzing fear, anxiety and panic, it has to be a deliberate on purpose action. I know that if I could overcome these hurtles, you certainly can! Let's move on to the next step.

Chapter Six

DETERMINATION

The Discipline for Change

Tony Robbins is one of my long term mentors. I have listened to and read his material for years. In his book, <u>Awaken the Giant Within</u>, he talks about the force that impacts every facet of our lives and that is **PAIN and PLEASURE.** Everything you and I do, we do it either out of our need to avoid pain or our desire to gain pleasure. And your determination in life is often the gauge whether you are going to experience pain or pleasure.

Determination is what gives you the advantage in life to move forward. And it is what keeps you motivated to change. It is fear of something bad or the anticipation of something great which really causes us to go for it or remain the same. Determination is the breakfast for champions, and if you can discipline yourself I believe that you will win in life and defeat fear, panic, and anxiety to reach your ultimate success.

Building Life With the Storm in Mind

An ancient script says, "In life you will have trouble." Storms, disappointments, setbacks, and all sorts of unexpected things will come. These are the issues that tend to throw our lives off balance, which can send us over the edge into the fear of the unknown. If you are reading this book; perhaps, you can identify with having multiple storms in your life. The second part of the ancient script says, "Cheer up because you have hope!"

There is always hope regardless of how bad the storm may be.

Here is the mindset. We already know that life is going to share some storms with us, but as we build our lives, it would be wise to build with the storm in mind. If you can create a predetermined action to the unexpected events in life, it will help you stay balanced to keep you from being thrown off of your course. However, it will require discipline and commitment. I would love to tell you that it is easy, but it is not. That is the simple truth, but here's the power of discipline. You get to chose how you view your life's storm. Is it good or bad? The choice is yours. I chose to believe that every storm was an opportunity for me to build onto my conscience (belief system). I looked at it as a development tool because without it I would not have become better.

Now, I must say that I don't like storms, but I refuse to allow the storm to weather me. I choose to weather it. It is your mindset in life that will help you overcome fear, panic, and anxiety, so that you can experience **success in life**!

GETTING BACK TO YOU COACHING TIP

Make the choice to weather the storm instead of letting the storm weather you

Most of us have been conditioned in life that when problems come, we should worry. Or when we are startled, we should be afraid. As well, when we get upset, we should blow up. All of these are preconditioned emotional responses that can be reprogrammed to be positive and constructive responses.

I mentioned at the beginning of the book that I cared for both of my parents, and they died while I was in my thirties. I remember prior to their death that I would reason with myself and condition my mind to accept the fact that my parents are going to die one day. My dad was in his eighties and my mother had cancer for many years, so at some point, I knew she was going to die. So, I embraced the fact that death is a part of life and I had to let them go. When they died, I grieved like everyone else, but I did not "fall to pieces" because I already conditioned my mind for this. This was a storm in my life for sure, but I learned to build life with the storm in mind. For more information on how to deal with anxiety and panic associated with death, please visit my website at: **www.tyronlister.com**.

I know that admitting and accepting that some things are out of your control may be difficult to do, but the truth of the matter is that this is the process of life. It is liberating to know that you do not have to carry the weight of the world on your shoulders. The results of change are realized through determination. When life throws you a curve ball, pick up the bat and knock it out of the ballpark. It's okay to cry. It's okay to be angry. It's okay to be upset. But no matter what, be determined to get back to YOU!

Why

In a previous chapter, I talked about your WHY? In this section I will show you how to define your why and how to dig deep into your soul to discover the true reason that you want to make a change in your life. Your why will push you when you feel like giving up and going back to what is familiar. It is the framework that establishes the structure for your come back.

When you are defining your why there are a few things that will help you that you should consider:

1. Your why has to be bigger than you.
2. Your why has to touch you to the point where you can't live without it.
3. Your why should move you in every area of your soul (mind, will,

imagination, emotions, and intellect).

In the words of the great motivational speaker, Les Brown, "You've got to be hungry." You've got to want it so bad that when you are in the heat of battle and every opposing force is against you, you won't quit! This is what it is going to take to defeat fear, panic, and anxiety in order to get back to you.

Here are steps to frame your why:

1. Find your target – What are you aiming for?

_____
_____
_____
_____
_____

2. Take Action equal to that target – For example, if you want to defeat fear, then don't watch scary movies, but rather create a positive fear-free atmosphere.

_____
_____
_____
_____
_____

3. Set realistic goals that will get you to your why – Give a realistic time frame like three months, six months or a year. Unrealistic goals will cause you to lose heart in the process and give up because you feel that you can never reach them.

_____
_____
_____
_____
_____

4. Now ask yourself why do I want this? Do you really want to be free from fear, panic, and anxiety? This is the type of question you want to ask.

_____
_____
_____
_____
_____

5. Why do you want to be free from fear, panic, and anxiety? (i.e. I have to stay inside because I get too anxious when I go outside because of this condition and I want to go outside).

_____
_____
_____
_____
_____

6. Why do you want to go outside? Because I enjoy taking long walks. It helps me clear my head and find my focus.

_____
_____
_____
_____
_____

This is the pattern to use in asking yourself why? The more you ask why to your why, the more defined it becomes, which will move you from just an initial surface answer to the core of why you want to make this change.

When your why is compelling enough that is makes you cry or makes you upset that you don't have it, then you will push yourself to get it. Determination is a disciplined mindset that says, "I won't stop at anything before I get it."

During this process, know that you will have to revisit your why often until you reach your desired goal.

GETTING BACK TO YOU COACHING TIP

Be angry. Be upset. But be determined to Get Back to YOU!

The Breaking Point

I have come to far to turn around now

The breaking point is the place where you get to in your journey where you will either have a break down or breakthrough. You may have experienced this point in life already if you are reading this book. Layers of hurt, unresolved emotional issues, constant lies and repeated let downs packaged with stress and the lack of rest can bring you to a breaking point. I remember my doctor told me that my type of anxiety disorder was a result of years of unresolved issues, and all it was going to take was one small thing to push me over the edge. It would have been the proverbial straw that broke the camel's back.

Just as the doctor said, I did reach that point and my breaking point sent me into a six month spiral of frustration, but I was determined that I was not going to live that way for the rest of my life.

You may be at your breaking point right now or you can see signs of it coming. The good news is that you do not have to remain in your condition. Your life has a meaning. You have a purpose and the truth is this is not your quitting time. By all means, you have come too far to "throw in the towel" now. It's time to push pass your breaking point and break through! The methods that I am sharing with you in this book will help you move pass a life of fear, panic, and anxiety to live a life of **freedom and success!**

Positive Affirmation: *I'm not going back. I'm moving ahead. I align my life with my why, and I am moving forward!*

Chapter Seven

EXPECTATION

The Belief in Change

The atmosphere of expectancy is the breeding ground of miracles

~Rod Parsley

A Persian legend tells us that a certain king needed a faithful servant to serve in his palace, and had to choose between two candidates for the office. He took both at fixed wages and told them to fill a basket with water from a nearby well and in the evening time he would return to inspect their work. After dumping one or two buckets of water into the basket, one of the men said, "What is the good of doing this useless work? As soon as we pour the water in, it runs out the sides." The other answered, "But we have our wages, haven't we? The use is the master's business, not ours." "I'm not going to do such fool's work," replied the complainer. Throwing down his bucket, he went away.

The other man continued until he had drained the well. Looking down into it, he saw something shining at the bottom that proved to be a diamond ring. "Now I see the use of pouring water into the basket!" he exclaimed. "If the bucket had brought up the ring before the well was dry, it would have been found in the basket. Our work was not useless."

When blessings and good things do not fully coincide with your expectations in life, remember to wait until the well is dry. There may be something more precious at the bottom.

GETTING BACK TO YOU COACHING TIP

Faith + Applied Efforts= Results

As you move through this process from this point on, your spiritual makeup and condition will also play a vital role. This is a very critical step in your getting back to you process. This is where you connect your applied efforts with your spiritual faith. There will be gaps in the process and at times you will need help and this is where your spirituality will help you. I must say that the building blocks for me were consecration, information, saturation, deliberation, and determination, but the foundation was my expectation. You see, after I went through all of the steps over and over again, I recognized that it was my spiritual life that helped me move forward and be free from fear, panic and anxiety. Expectation is where you put your hope into action.

Faith without corresponding action is absolutely dead. – James the brother of greatness

You may not be a spiritual person and this section may not mean much to you, but I encourage you not to pass over it. Because when you are gripped by a paralyzing hold that makes you a slave to fear, panic and anxiety, you need a miracle to help you change your life and experience success in every area. Let's continue.

Proven Principles That Work

A principle works whether you work it or not. It works whether you believe it or not. Based on this fact, it is important to follow principles that have been proven to get results in the areas of life that you need results. Here is an example. Let's use the principle of sowing and reaping. If you have a radish seed and you plant it in the ground, wait about 30 days and you will get a radish in return for your seed that you planted. This is a principle also know as a law and this law is irrefutable. When you follow principles that work, then you have the right to expect something in return.

In this book, I have shared several principles that have been proven and I know that if you follow them, you will experience similar results. The glue that holds it all together is expectation.

Expectation has much to do with your conscience mind (your belief system), which is the foundation of what we build our lives upon. What you believe about yourself and your future will determine what you do today to create that future. I believe that every person should live free from any type of panic, fear, and anxiety that controls and paralyzes them from living a successful life.

The Future Now Showing

After being in the people business for over 25 years, I have recognized that some people experience fear and anxiety because of unproductive relationships. Many times these relationships are toxic and detrimental to the successful future that an individual may desire.

For different reasons people give others the power to alter their future when in reality most people are going along with the other person because they don't want to be alone or some other emotional needs that is being filled. After a while you notice that this is not the life that you desired nor is it the person you desired to be. In essence, you have followed someone else's expectation and hoped that they would eventually see it your way.

GETTING BACK TO YOU COACHING TIP

Your current condition is not an indication of your future potential

Now, you feel trapped because you don't want to hurt the other person's feelings. I call this "hopium," meaning that in this case hope is not pure, but it is like a drug that keeps you stuck in a situation that continues to trigger bad emotions and negative responses. I know for some, this may seem a little rough and straightforward, but my remedy for hopium is to get a backbone and live *your* dreams and not someone else's. The greatest freedom that I ever experienced in life was the freedom from other people's opinion of me.

You have the power and potential to create the type of future that you desire -- one of freedom, fulfillment and fun. If you need to reread chapter three to recapture your vision to make it happen; then I recommend that you do it. Your future may seem foggy and doubtful right now, but you can create any kind of future you desire. You just have to want it bad enough. I know that if I could overcome these disorders that I had (fear, panic and anxiety) to live a successful life of freedom, you can, too.

GETTING BACK TO YOU COACHING TIP

> You have the power and potential to create the type of future that you desire

The good news is that you don't have to wait for a special day or some special event. You can start creating that future right now. The title of this section reminds me of a movie theatre that previews coming attractions and before the previews start there is an image and a voice that says, "The Future Now Showing." Go ahead and let's play your preferred future on the canvas of your imagination. You deserve it! It will be fun, but also it will help you shift your mind from your current situation to your future possibilities.

As you play this high definition video in your imagination repeatedly, it starts to affect your belief system because now you believe that you can have that future. It's like you can live it, and own it!

Believe

When you believe you can make the impossible possible; then the impossible can be possible.

Belief is what pushes you to go beyond the surface and dig into the possibilities. If you have belief, then you can move mountains and do amazing things you never thought possible. Like **Lance Armstrong,** who was a world-renowned cyclist who overcame testicular cancer. He was told that his chance of survival was 40%, but against the odds, he beat cancer and went on to win seven consecutive Tour de France medals.

Or, **Elizabeth Blackwell** who was blind in one eye and was the first woman to receive a medical degree in the United States, as well as the first woman on the UK Medical Register in the mid 1800's. She was the first openly identified woman to graduate from medical school, a pioneer in promoting the education of women in medicine in the United States, and a social and moral reformer in both the United States and in England.

Getting Back To You

When you believe in yourself against the odds, there is a dynamic that happens and I can't explain it, but it causes you to go farther and propel you to do more than you could ever imagine. When you believe in yourself and the source that flows through you, YOU will be unstoppable. I had the belief that I could overcome paralyzing panic attacks, and I did it! So my question to you is what can you do if you believe? I encourage you to believe in your success more than you can breathe. Believe that it is possible for you. Believe that you deserve to live a life of freedom. Expect it to happen. Close off any other options in your mind against your success, and watch what happens. Now Go Do It!

Chapter Eight

MANIFESTATION

The Results of Change

When you are fighting the type of disorders like I overcame, you know upfront and personal how these abnormalities can affect your life. Even though it is a psychological issue, it has very real physical implications. In addition to dealing with the affects of each of these emotional mayhems, many people deal with embarrassment and shame that is attached to these psychological disorders. Also, some have difficulty dealing with the fact that during this time, they feel like they have no control over their situation.

Another challenge is trying to explain their condition to someone who has no frame of reference for what they are experiencing. From literal physical pains that come with this issue to being tortured by what you are fighting everyday is a very difficult experience.

GETTING BACK TO YOU COACHING TIP

Your experience is never at the mercy of someone else's criticism

Because of this paralyzing lifestyle, deep down inside most people just want to break free from this and move forward with their lives. This is the desire you want to draw from to push you to get the results that you desire, no matter what!

The word manifestation according to the online dictionary means an indication of the existence, reality, or presence of something. It literally means that what you desire, you now have. This is such a wonderful thought because after you have suffered with panic, fear, and anxiety along with putting forth your earnest effort to apply the principles of this book to your life, the success is well deserved.

Pleasure Out Of Pain

It seems unreal at times that the intense pain that you may be experiencing would have a positive future. It seems unreal that you can actually help someone else while championing your own situation. I remember when my doctor suggested that I write a book about how I overcame my situation and help someone else, I was amazed because I realized at that moment, I overcame what I was dealing with. I actually experienced pleasure from a painful situation. I went to restaurants that I could not go to previously. I watched a movie at the movie theatre. I drove my vehicle for long distances. I flew on airplanes. I could do things alone! That was a big one for me. All of these activities that my condition prohibited me from doing; I found pleasure in being able to do them again.

Our light afflictions which are but for a moment works for us.

~Paul the Apostle

What a relief to know that I was back to life! Because of this experience, I now have a much sweeter perspective on life and I take advantage of every pleasurable moment because I remember when there were no pleasurable moments. I would not have chosen this path in life, but since I have traveled this road, I can say thank you to the experience because it made me who I am today. You may be thinking that what I am talking about seems so far away and you may be wondering if this is possible for you. I know because it seemed that way for me for a while. My encouragement to you is, don't give up because you will experience freedom from this unpleasant lifestyle, if you don't quit. The only way that you can fail is if you stop. Keep moving step by step, principle by principle, and you will see the results that you desire.

GETTING BACK TO YOU COACHING TIP

You are designed to take advantage of life's pleasurable moments, so that you can champion the non-pleasurable moments

Through The Valley

Yea though I walk through the valley of the shadow of death.

~Psalm 23

My grandmother taught this Psalm to me when I was a little boy and I have treasured it ever since. When I was dealing with fear in my life, this Psalm was a point of solace for me. Almost every night, I would be kept awake because of the fear of death. It caused me to be on edge often and when I would hyperventilate grasping for each breath as if it was my last, the fear of dying would grip me. This was a vicious cycle because each short breath was squeezed out by a serious fear that each breath was my last. On and on it went day after day, and it got worse at night. When I started walking through the process that I am sharing in this book, it was still very bad. As I would rehearse in my mind, "I am walking **through** the valley of the shadow of death," I was able to shift my mind.

The key word here is – through -- I was no longer looking at death as a villain, but as a natural process of life. I was not ready to die, but along this journey, I wasn't afraid of it anymore. Remembering this Psalm helped me realize that what I was experiencing was not death, it was simply a shadow.

A shadow is cast because of a larger more brilliant light shinning against an object. The comfort that I have is that death may be in this valley, but my focus is on the larger light. It was my belief in that light that helped me walk through my valley.

GETTING BACK TO YOU COACHING TIP

Life's valleys are designed to help you reach deeper inside yourself so that you can become the person that you were designed to be. What you learn in the valley can change your life.

Perhaps, you are still thinking that this spiritual section of this book is not for you, and trust me I am in no way trying to impose my beliefs on you, all I am doing is simply sharing with you the secrets to my success. You may be able to follow the other steps in this book and recover on your own, and I applaud you. For me, it was my spiritual foundation that created the success that I desired, and have been able to maintain every since. If you are feeling overwhelmed with fear, panic, and anxiety, focus on this simple truth, you are just passing through the valley, and not going to the valley. It helps shift your mind.

I Did It

When I was growing up, I loved to figure things out. I would spend hours putting together puzzles or trying to accomplish some task that I was learning. One of the greatest memories that I have of those times in my life is the feeling of... **I Did It!** So it was these formative years that I adopted the mindset – I can do it! More than accomplishing the task was the feeling that came along with accomplishing the task. It was that "I did it!" feeling. Because of this resolve, I have been able to accomplish things that in my mind seemed impossible.

Here's the deal. If I can do it, **SO CAN YOU!** I am not better than you and I did not have a special package deal to help me succeed. I found a method that works and then I worked my but off to get the results that I desired. If you are willing to put in the effort you will get the results. Let me leave you with this little coaching tip that helped me develop this mindset as a little boy and I hope it will inspire you, too.

GETTING BACK TO YOU COACHING TIP

Bite off more than you can chew and chew it. Take on more than you can bear and bear it. Don't let life champion you.
Champion LIFE!

Chapter Nine

CELEBRATION

The Accomplishment of Change

One of my goals was to maintain and keep my balance in my life. I adopted the philosophy years ago that if you work hard, you should play hard. Life is a precious gift that we have been given and what we put into it will determine the quality that we get out of it. Panic attacks and anxiety took life out of me. It consumed my energy and emotions. After almost every episode, I had to lie down and rest because it drained me -- over and over again every day for months. That by itself was hard work and when you add that to the earnest effort it took to walk through the steps that I am sharing in this book, it took all that I had.

GETTING BACK TO YOU COACHING TIP

It takes earnest effort to achieve and maintain BALANCE and FOCUS.

Now, that I am living on the other side of THE BIG THREE, I recognize that this issue consumed a large chunk of my life. I worked hard to be an overcomer, and now that I have been able to live a successful life of freedom from this paralyzing condition, I take every moment that I can to celebrate life.

Party Time

Whether it's having dinner with friends, date night with my wife, quality time with my son, or serving people, I take every opportunity to have a party. The reason that I celebrate is because my life was literally shut down and almost taken away from me. Today, I live with an attitude of gratitude. With every smile and every hand shake, I am grateful that I can live life free from fear, panic and anxiety that ONCE controlled my life. I want you to understand that the big three (3) will always show up and be a part of life to some degree. In fact, you cannot live a balanced life without their presence at some point. The key is to use them as tools and as a sounding board for distinguishing between reality and perception instead of letting them control your life and use you. When I experienced their affects in my life, I immediately switch to celebration mode because I remember when those feeling and emotions would overtake me. And now, I can control them. What a liberating feeling!

This journey helped me realize that laughter is good for the soul. There is an ancient proverb that says, *"A merry heart does good like a medicine."* Laughter is a natural healer. According to naturalnews.com, laughter can increase your oxygen level; help with circulation and boost your immune system.

Laughter has many psychological benefits that help the quality of our lives. I know the getting back to YOU process can be difficult and quite challenging, but I suggest to you that for every accomplishment you achieve in this process that you take a moment and have a party and celebrate because you are getting back to YOU.

You

My doctor did not give me a medicinal remedy, instead she asked me, what I enjoy doing and told me to go do you. Sometimes life makes us believe that if we spend time or money on ourselves that we are being selfish and inconsiderate of others. Some even feel guilty for doing small things for themselves. To achieve a balance in life you must spend time "Doing You." This time could be spent having a quiet moment over a cup of hot tea, taking a walk to clear your mind, reading a book you enjoy, buying something for yourself, meditating and reading positive material, or just doing something recreational. Whatever you do, "do you."

GETTING BACK TO YOU COACHING TIP

> Helping others starts by helping YOU first.

For years, I have helped feed the hungry and less fortunate people around the world. One day it came to my mind that it would be impossible for me to help others with what they needed if I didn't have the resources to help them. During my getting back to you process, I refocused on this concept. If I don't take time for me, then I am not giving my optimal service to others. I am giving them what's left over. This is service at its lowest level. It's also life at its lowest level.

If you don't take time to replenish and refuel yourself, then at some point you will end up burned out and headed for a crash. That day, I felt like my doctor was giving me permission to spend time on me. In the same way I am saying to you, do what you enjoy. Spend some time doing you so that you can be refreshed and ready to live life at its highest level.

Pay It Forward

Gratitude is a powerful force of life. It is connected with a deep appreciation of what you have been given and is expressed in many different ways. One of the greatest ways to express gratitude is to pay it forward. According to Wikipedia Dictionary online, this phrase is defined as the concept of asking that a good deed be repaid by having it done for others instead of repayment to the creditor.

This book is my effort to pay it forward for the gift of life that I received again. Since my ordeal, my goal has been to make a living, living life and to make a living by giving. There are many times that I will give someone a coaching session at no charge or give a donation without looking for the credit. There are many ways to pay it forward and keep the blessings circulating. My request of you is that after you have finished *the getting back to you* process and you are living a life free from the big three (3), that you pay it forward and help someone else. If you join me in this effort, we can change the world, one boy, one girl, one person at a time, and help them live a life of freedom and success!

GETTING BACK TO YOU
COACHING TIP

Giving is Living

Chapter Ten

AFTERWARDS

What's Really Happening?

Wow! If you have already started the getting back to you process and you are at this chapter, you have come a long way. I want to congratulate you for your courage and fortitude to live your dream of freedom and success free from the big three (3). I am sure that there have been a lot of changes from chapter one until now, and you may be asking the question what's really happening. I am glad you asked.

If you have started this process, you have experienced many emotional, psychological, physical, and spiritual changes. You could possibly be tired from the process of change itself. But what is really happening is CHANGE. According to thefreedictionary.com the definition of change is: To cause to be different.

After you have followed the getting back to you process somewhere along your journey, you want to see change. You want to feel different. You want to be able to breathe again. You want to be able to live again. Ultimately, you want your life to be different. This is what is really happening.

Guilt and Embarrassment

I can't complete this book without talking about two of the major feelings that most people experience when dealing with fear, panic and anxiety. People feel guilty because of thoughts of letting down or disappointing someone they care about. People feel guilt because of the question; how could I let this happen? If your response to anxiety is irritability, or not being able to sleep in the same bed with your partner, you may have negative feelings about your situation.

Perhaps you feel guilty for feeling numb and detached and responding to others that way. These are all signs of anxiety. I was very irritable at times and when I was able to, I would often apologize to my family and ask them to forgive me.

In connection with guilt is embarrassment because most people don't want others to see them with this condition. My response to guilt and embarrassment is to use them as stepping stones to your freedom. Let them serve you instead of you serving them. All it requires is a change in perspective. Decide that you will no longer give guilt or embarrassment the power to control you. If you are reading this book, then you want to change. Keep that in mind when you feel guilty and embarrassed about what you are experiencing. Let this serve as motivation for you to change your situation.

Partners

It is important that you know that you are not in this alone. There are others that care about you and want to see you live a successful life free from the big three (3). I strongly encourage you to find a partner who is willing to help you walk through your recovery process.

GETTING BACK TO YOU COACING TIP

There is someone, somewhere waiting to help you Get Back to YOU

At the time when I decided that I was ready to get out of the house and try and experience some type or normalcy, I had a friend named Keith that would come over and pick me up and drive me around. I wasn't ready to drive yet, but this was my first big step. When he drove me around, he would play all the types of music that he knew I enjoyed. We would laugh and talk about funny things. We would sing and just have a blast doing nothing. He helped me learn how to feel comfortable eating in a restaurant and being in public social settings again.

One of the most importing things that he did, and I want you to pay attention to this section, is when he saw me get anxious and start the panic process, he would simply talk to me. I recognized that if I had someone tell me that I am okay and that it's going to be alright, I was able to control the panic attacks with the confidence in knowing that I was not alone. There were so many things that he helped me regain that it is impossible to explain it all. All I can say is thanks, Keith!

Find someone who can help walk you through the process. You can go to

www.tyronelister.com for more information on our coaching program. You are not alone and we will partner with you to help you walk through your process one step at a time.

Let It Go

Congratulations, you made it through the getting back to you process! The purpose is to go through the steps in the book as many times as you need to in order to achieve the level of success that you desire. The key word here is process.

Some will move through these steps fairly quickly and for others it may take some time. The goal is to help you let go of what has been holding you back from a life of freedom and success. With time and proper management of your emotions you, too, can let it go!

The journey of getting back to you is provoking, challenging, and sometimes scary, but nevertheless, it is often exciting and always powerful. The rewards you reap as a result of all your hard work will be well worth the time and effort you have devoted to this process. I hope that you will take the time now to acknowledge all that you have done because it's no small task. In fact, it is really BIG! We've covered a lot of ground, and you stuck with me, step-by-step, from beginning to end.

This is not the end. It is not even the beginning of the end. It is, perhaps the beginning of the end.

~Sir Winston Churchill

The steps that I have shared in this book are a marvelous path to your recover and the beginning of an incredible life free from fear, panic and anxiety. It may happen for you on any level of this process: Consecration, Information, Saturation, Deliberation, Determination, Expectation, Manifestation or Celebration. Or it could be something I said in the introduction or the last sentence of this book. Wherever it starts for you, embrace the moment. **Live it,**

Own it, and Champion it! The best person to get back to is YOU!

CONCLUSION

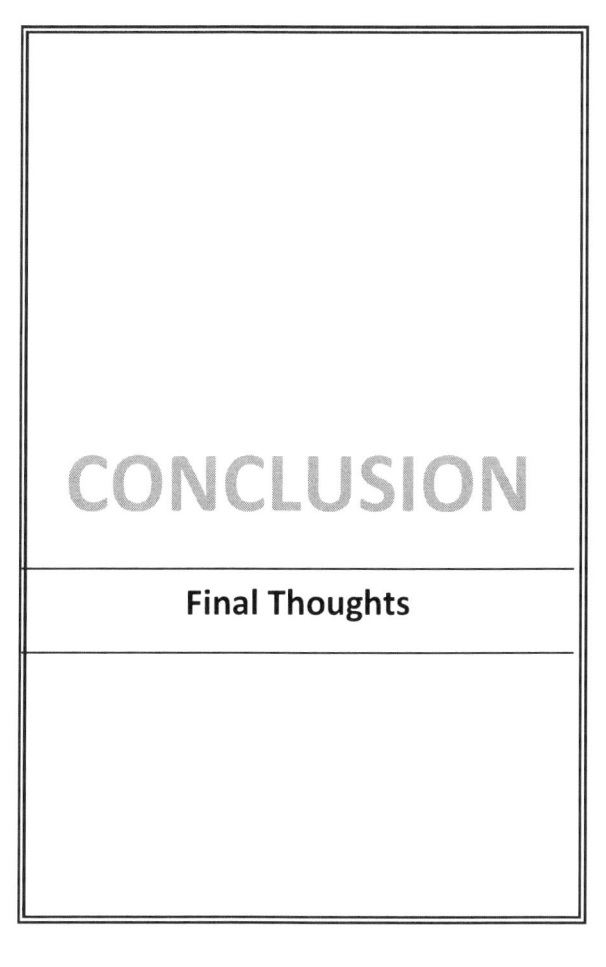

Final Thoughts

Getting Back To You

YOU DID IT! YOU FINISHED WHAT YOU STARTED, AND I AM BEYOND PROUD of you for that accomplishment. Here is what to do next.

1. **Go back and reread this book** and complete the exercises. There is too much packed in the book for you to have picked it up the first go-around. Repetition is the mother of all skill, so go back over this book, especially the chapters that gave you the most aha

moments. Take the time to go back over the things you have skipped over.

2. **Apply what you have learned** and take action on the many things you have written down. Throughout this book you have acquired a lot of information and knowledge some new and some old information presented in a new or different way. Regardless of that, now that you have the knowledge, you must turn it into power through your action steps. Visit my website to learn more about various coaching resources that I recommend; also check out the informational page following this chapter to learn more about the many wonderful coaching opportunities that www.Tyronelister.com has to offer.

3. **Send me an e-mail** to gettingback2you@gmail.com and let me know how this book has changed your

life. Most authors write books and never look back on the real difference that the book made in the lives of the people who read it. I want you to share with me how this book has impacted your life, your family, your business, and your destiny!

4. **Share this book and its impact with others** whom you know and love. If this book has been a blessing to your life in a major way, why keep it a secret? Tell your friends, family, co-workers, and neighbors. Form book clubs and special "YOU" empowerment groups to study the material at deeper levels. Encourage as many people as you can to go online or to their nearest bookstore to buy this book today!

You've read the book, NOW WHAT?

Join Tyrone's Getting Back To YOU Coaching Program

This book has deposited many principles, strategies, ideas, and concepts inside of you. Now let Tyrone and his team of highly trained professionals help get what's inside of you, out! Tyrone has been your coach through this book, now let him coach you through your Getting Back to YOU process!

The most successful people in the world, from business to entertainment, from government to sports, from academia to ministry; all have one thing in common. They all have coaches; people who help them to become all that they were designed and created to be.

Now is your opportunity to continue along your path of Getting Back to YOU with the help of Tyrone, his highly trained team, and his powerful new coaching program designed just for you.

To learn more and register now, visit
www.TyroneLister.com

Notes:

Mental toughness for Success
Dr. IV Hilliard (1996 Light Publishing)

The Confidence Makeover
Dr. Keith Johnson (2006 Destiny Image Publishers, Inc.)

Caught Between a Dream and a Job
Delatorro McNeal II (Excel Books 2008)

Dictionary.com

Wikipedia.com

Made in the USA
San Bernardino, CA
28 March 2015